Writing to Make a DIFFERENCE

How to share your message and secure your legacy by writing a nonfiction book

The Visionary Library Book 2

by

TONY ROGERS JR.

Published by Visionary Press
©2018 Tony Rogers Jr.
All rights reserved

No portion of this publication may be reproduced, stored in any electronic system or transmitted in any form or by any means, electronic, mechanical, photocopy, recording or otherwise, without written permission from the author. Brief quotations maybe used in literary reviews.

Connect with Tony: thevisionarysocietyinfo@gmail.com

"To be remembered beyond death, write something worth reading or do something worth writing about."

– Benjamin Franklin

CONTENTS

Introduction 1

CHAPTER 1 - The Power of a Book 5

CHAPTER 2 - Preparing to Write 15

CHAPTER 3 - Beginning to Write 21

CHAPTER 4 - How to Publish Your Book 29

Conclusion 37

About the Author 39

Other books from the author 41

INTRODUCTION

Do you have a burning desire to share your message with the world? Do you have a message of hope, healing, or inspiration you want to get out to the masses? Using the medium of writing to touch the lives of others is not relegated to a select few. It is accessible and practical for anyone with a clear message, an insatiable desire to share that message, and an understanding of some fundamental principles.

Documenting and preserving your thoughts in print is one of the most important undertakings you can attempt. With each stroke of your keypad you are crafting a written legacy that has the potential to positively impact lives for generations to come. As a person with the desire to make a difference in the world, this idea may be motivating yet fill you with a healthy dose of fear. You may think (as I did), "I want to write a book, but I don't know how," or, "I'm not a writer so how can I write a book?" " Your questions and concerns may be numerous, yet in the coming pages we will address these and many other objections to the writing process.

You will learn:

- How your ideas, discoveries, and unique life experiences can be used to make a difference in the world.
- Why anyone with a message and a strong desire to share that message can (and should) write a book.
- Why getting your message in print is one of the most efficient ways to expand the potential reach and impact of your message.
- A step-by-step process for getting a quality book written and out to the world.

My Decision to Write

For my entire adult life, I've wanted to write a book. Not because I loved to write or had any particular skill in the craft, but because I wanted to use my ideas to help people on a large scale. Internal battles with fear left that desire a dream for six years before it became a reality. My first bit of advice? Don't let this happen to you! It took me six years to write my first book, and less than eight months to write two more.

What changed? I made a decision! Motivational legend Tony Robbins has an excellent quote that reads, "A real decision is measured by the fact that you've taken a new action. If there's no action, you haven't truly decided." The following decisions changed the direction of my life and legacy forever.

1. My decision to study the writing process.

   The "perfected" look of a finished book can be intimidating when you're not quite sure of the process it took to create that state. Studying the process demystified and distilled it into learnable steps that gave me the confidence I needed to get started. As we move forward, I will share with you the best practices I've learned from hours of study and tweaking my personal writing process along the way.

2. My decision to write in spite of my fear.

   The hardest part about writing my first book was getting over my fear about writing my first book. It will be the same for you. Our doubts about the validity of our message and perceived inadequacies as a writer keeps us bound more than any other factor. Doubt is an ever-present enemy of writing. Battles with self-doubt are universal to every writer's journey at different levels and to varying degrees. You will never completely silence doubt, nor do you need to. You must learn to write in spite of its presence. This takes discipline, diligence, and most of all, a firm decision to do so.

Chapter **1**

THE POWER OF A BOOK

Has reading a book changed your life? It has mine. In fact, I would submit to you that virtually every book you have read has made a difference in your life in some way. Maybe it gave you a new perspective, helped you push a little harder towards your goals, or even coached you through a major life crisis. Although that book improved the quality of your life, did you personally know the author? Does the author reside in your city? State? Country, even? In many cases the answer to these questions are no, hence the power of a book. A book is much more than ink, paper, and glue; it is an instrument of change. Writing a book earns you the opportunity and privilege to influence the life of someone you will probably never meet.

To really drive this point home, here are five reasons why I believe books are one of the most important tools for social change we have access to:

1. A book is an extension of its author, allowing the author to be a teacher, guide, or mentor beyond their physical presence. Your book will never get tired or call in sick. It is always eager to teach on your behalf while you are doing other things.
2. A book allows the author to have influence beyond their physical death. Their thoughts have the potential to affect change for future generations to come. A perfect example of this is a great book I often re-read titled *The Law of Success* by Napoleon Hill. This book was originally published in 1928 and is still making a difference in the lives of thousands of readers today. The author's legacy is secure through this and his many other works.
3. A book can mobilize a movement, revolutionize an industry, or cause a paradigm shift in the culture, leading to rapid personal and social change. This has happened many times in almost every conceivable sector of society such as health, economics, science, human behavior, education, and spirituality.
4. A book allows us to pass a metaphorical baton of ideas to others, providing seeds of knowledge and experience that they can consume and build on. Learning from and improving on the discoveries of others is how the human race advances forward. All great ideas, books, or businesses were built on the shoulders of those that came before it.
5. One of the indirect ways a book can help create change is that it can give the reader permission to write a book of their own. A reader may be inspired by a book which will spark the desire in them to want to

do the same for others. Many authors report that their reading experiences is largely what gave them a desire to write. Your book could do the same for someone else.

Are you beginning to understand why you MUST write? As you can see, there is great power in a book, YOUR book!

Finding Your Message

Now that we've covered the WHY of getting your book written, let's dive into the practical HOW-TO. Our first stop in this process is to figure out the topic or message of your book. To do this you'll need to know the answers to the following three questions.

- Who do you want to talk to?
- What problem do you want to solve for your readers?
- What is your solution?

You probably already have a general idea of what each answer could be, but since these answers will form the basis of the material for your book, absolute clarity is essential.

1. Who do you want to talk to?

    This question is about defining your ideal reader – the special segment of society you want to speak to. No product is created for everyone. They each have their own predetermined target consumer. A book is no different. One of the biggest mistakes people make when trying to write a book is that *they try to write for too many people.* By trying to fulfill the needs of too many readers, you end up with a book that lacks the focus and depth to satisfy anyone.

Take some time to think about the type of person you want to read your book. Each attribute is important because they determine how you will craft your message. Everything – from the words you use to the specific examples and stories you share – will be based on your ideal reader's individual attributes. Begin with the prompts that follow but don't limit yourself there.

- What type of person would most benefit from reading your book?
- What is the gender of your ideal reader?
- What is the age range of your ideal reader?
- What is the educational background of your ideal reader?
- Does your ideal reader have a religious or secular background?
- Are there any experiences or specific beliefs your ideal reader should have to help them understand your message?

Some questions may not apply to your book topic and there is nothing wrong with that. These are only written as possible examples.

2. What problem do you want to solve for your readers?

The primary goal of a nonfiction book is to improve the lives of its readers – more specifically, to solve a problem for them. A reader is drawn to a nonfiction book based on the problem they perceive it will solve.

For example, you are reading this book because you want to learn how to get your message out to the world in the form of a book. That was the problem this book promised to solve, prompting you to read it. If I satisfy your needs by presenting a clear, actionable solution to this problem, you are likely to recommend it to others who have the same problem.

Understanding this is the key to writing a book that provides your readers with the most value. Whether you promise to help them overcome depression, increase their productivity, or become a better leader, everything depends on how well your solution helps them achieve their specific goal. In the eyes of your readers, the success of your nonfiction book will be measured on how well it solves their specific problem. What problem will your book attempt to solve for its readers?

3. What is your solution?

   As a nonfiction book author, you are a problem solver and your book is your solution in printed form. Providing this solution is how you reward the reader for investing their time and financial resources into your book. There are other books in the marketplace that will claim to offer the same solution as your book, but not from your unique perspective. Your unique perspective and experiences make your message unlike any other. The next few chapters are dedicated to providing you with my step-by-step process for getting your "solution" in print. As you begin to think about the solution you will provide, ask yourself these questions:

- Why should people read my book? What's in it for them?
- What is the desired result I want for my readers?
- What new knowledge would I like them to walk away with after reading my book?
- What examples or experiences can I use from my personal life to help explain my solution?
- How did I become an authority on this topic? How have I earned credibility?
- How will my book be different from other books on the same topic?

Your ideal reader + Your reader's problem + Your solution = Your message

When you know whose life you want to improve, or whose pain you want to heal, you've found your ideal reader. When you know what experience you want to share, or what truth you want to impart, you've found your message.

The Key Elements of a Nonfiction Book

There are six key elements that great nonfiction books have in common. Three focus on the content of the book and three focus on the character of its author. I group them into two separate categories which I call Heart and Mind.

Heart – Gratitude for the reader, a passion for your subject, authenticity

Mind – Clarity, structure, utility

Heart refers to the emotional core and unique personality of the author, while Mind refers to the way they structure and communicate ideas. A great nonfiction book is written with a combination of both. Heart without Mind has no practical value. It is motivational yet void of practical application. Mind without Heart is dry and passionless. It is empty of spirit and unable to connect with the reader.

Heart

1. Gratitude for the reader

   The first and most important element is to *genuinely feel* grateful for the reader and your opportunity to help them. This attitude permeates the entire project, becoming evident in the quality of your work. This doesn't mean your efforts will be perfect. It means that you will do everything you can to provide a good experience for your readers.

   I heard a story about Og Mandino, celebrated author of the mega bestseller, *The Greatest Salesman in the World.* He was asked why his books were so easy to read. He answered, "My books are so easy to read because they're so hard to write." They went on to say he sometimes rewrites his books nine or ten times before having them published. That level of work ethic only comes from a man who deeply cares about his readers and his craft. Genuinely caring about the receivers of your work is a prerequisite for producing good work.

2. A passion for your subject

    Let's face it, writing is hard work! In order to get your book written, you're going to need passion. Passion is the emotional energy you receive from a deep love and interest in your message. Passionate authors believe that there is value in their message. This belief leads to a burning desire to share it and the reader picks up on that passion as they consume the message.

    An inspired reader is the result of an inspired author. If you are not emotionally involved in your writing, don't expect the reader to be. Beloved author and poet Robert Frost said it best: "Any writing that calls on the reader's feelings must first call on the authors. No tears in the writer, no tears in the reader."

3. Authenticity

    The message you have to share with the world is your gift to the world. It is sacred. It is uniquely your own. As the sole keeper of this message, you have the responsibility to maintain its integrity. To deliver it to us in its purest form.

    You must have the courage to share your truth, just as you see it, knowing that others may disagree with or not see the value in what you have to say. Readers want your unbridled truth. The people for whom your message most resonates will appreciate and celebrate your authenticity.

Mind

Since writing is about communicating your thoughts via words, the quality of that communication must be your top priority. This is why the next three elements are indispensable to any writing process, especially when writing a complete book.

1. Clarity

    The bulk of your work as a writer will be spent crafting your words for clarity. This element is why we take on the painful process of re-writing, polishing, and editing. These lengthy processes thoroughly test the extent of our drive to complete a quality project.

2. Structure

    As a nonfiction writer, you are essentially a hired guide, leading the reader along the path of understanding a given subject. One of the ways you aid this process is the order in which you present your ideas. Knowledge is best understood, and therefore must be taught, in logical, sequential steps. Brick by brick, layer by layer, each new concept building on the others as you go.

3. Utility

    Not only do we want our readers to understand our ideas, we want them to apply those ideas in their everyday lives. You can't make your readers take action, but the tools they need to do so should be readily available if they decide to implement your advice. We all know the frustration of being presented with a great idea without the necessary information needed to execute it. Thoroughly presenting the "what" of an idea without the practical "how-to" is one of the greatest sins a nonfiction author can commit. Information is only as valuable as its ability to be used.

These are the key components needed to produce a quality nonfiction book. In no way do you need to be an expert at these before you begin (I certainly am not), but you do need to keep them in mind as you write and focus on getting better at them as you gain more experience.

Chapter 2

PREPARING TO WRITE

Writing a book is not for the fainthearted. For this reason, many people will never see their words in print. Writing is difficult for every author. It is a mentally and emotionally draining task that will thoroughly test your resolve to become an author. There is nothing that will make your process easy, but there are things you can do to make it more palatable.

I have five pre-writing rituals that help me prepare to tackle a new project. Some focus on my attitude and psychological approach to writing, while others help expand my base of knowledge specific to the book I am preparing to work on. As you gain more experience with your writing process you will develop unique pre-writing strategies of your own, but for now, I invite you to try my approach.

1. Don't try to write a book; instead, have a conversation.

   Although I have written five books, I don't consider myself to be a "writer." I am a teacher who chooses to use the medium of writing to share my ideas with the world. My first book was extremely hard for me to write because I was approaching it as a writer instead a teacher. Since I am a teacher by nature, making this distinction in my approach has made the process flow more naturally for me.

   As a teacher, I approach every writing project as a conversation with someone who seeks my mentorship on a topic. Each new book is simply another conversation on a different topic of mutual interest. As a result of reading the previous chapter, you (hopefully) described your ideal reader in detail; this is the person you want to write your book to.

   When you sit down to write, imagine this person asking questions about the subject of your book. This positions you as the teacher and begins a figurative question-and-answer session that forms the content of your book. Write your book as if you were teaching someone about your topic, because you are. How would you begin? What is the first thing they need to learn? What is the second? And so on.

   I did this exercise with a friend of mine over lunch last week. He has always wanted to write a book but didn't know how to get started. He is a fitness coach who loves to help people get in great physical shape, so I figured the subject of his book would focus on that. I told him I believed he already knew his book topic and the content that needed to be inside that book. He said he didn't think so, but he was open to the challenge.

I asked him, "What message do you want to bring to the world?"

He immediately said, "Living a happy and healthy lifestyle."

I said, "Good! Maybe, 'How to live a happy and healthy lifestyle' could be the title." He smiled. I then asked, "From your perspective, what exactly does 'living a happy and healthy lifestyle' mean?"

He paused to collect his thoughts and answered, "It means for your body to be consistently functioning at its best. This includes your energy levels, internal organs, and even how you think."

Then I prompted further thought by asking, "How does someone go about starting this lifestyle? What are the top five-to-seven things they need to do?" I explained to him that his answers to this question could easily supply the individual chapters for his book. In about 15 minutes of questions and answers, we had a rough idea of what his book title and chapters would be. He wrote it all down and I left our lunch together inspired and grateful for the experience.

My friend already knew the content for his book; he just needed someone to help him bring what he knew to the surface by asking a few stimulating questions. If you don't have someone to help you do this, try the next best thing – which is *using your imagination*. This is what I do every time I sit down to write.

2. Believe that getting your message out is your calling

    Each new writing project is extremely important to me because my work is tied to my life's purpose. I believe that I was given each message as a calling. As such, it is my responsibility to get these messages out to the world. They don't benefit anyone if I selfishly and irresponsibly hold them inside. They need to be consumed and appreciated by others for my mission to be complete.

    I don't write because I *want* to write. I write because I *MUST* write. Having this mindset helps me stay focused and push through when things get tough. Thinking about your writing in a similar manner will do the same for you.

3. Read other books in your genre.

    Your book idea begins as a fragile seed of inspiration that must mature before it is solid enough to document in a book. This evolution process takes time, personal experience, and reflection. However, you can speed up this process by learning from the experiences of others.

    I read a minimum of ten books on a subject before I will consider writing a book on it. My goal is to have my current knowledge challenged and strengthened by great authors that came before me.

    Reading books in your genre also gives you a competitive advantage because you get to see what other writers have done well and where they may have dropped the ball. You can use this vital marketplace information to create a product that serves your readers better.

4. Have something with you to document any new ideas you receive.

   Ideas and words are priceless to a writer and should be treated as such. A good idea or phrase can appear in your mind at any time and you must be ready to capture it immediately. I've been known to excuse myself during a conversation or even jump out of bed in the middle of the night to quickly document a new idea. I've learned the hard way that despite my best efforts and level of inspiration at the moment, I won't remember my new idea very long.

   Some authors like to use portable audio recorders to capture their loose ideas. Others use pen and paper. I started off with pen and paper, but I would often lose the little slips of paper. I found using a notepad app on my smart phone that organized and saved all my information was the best way to keep track of my ideas.

   Train yourself to collect phrases, quotes, and other ideas you come across that pertain to your book. This will make your writing experience easier when you begin because much of your book will already be written in your notes. It will just be a matter of putting things in their proper order and expanding on the ideas you have captured.

5. Study the craft of writing.

   As I mentioned earlier, I don't consider myself to be a writer, but I do respect the craft of writing. This is why – before I wrote a single word – I studied many classic and contemporary books on writing. The book that helped me the most, and the one I refer to often, is *On Writing Well* by William Zinsser. Do yourself a favor and read this book twice before you begin writing your first book. It will help your writing in ways you'll appreciate later.

Chapter 3

BEGINNING TO WRITE

I don't personally know you or what your book will be about, but I do know this: writing your book will be an emotional roller coaster. You will go through many unpredictable highs and lows of emotion. Your inner critic and inner hero will engage in unrelenting combat until the very last word is typed. This is the grueling work of an author that our readers never see, and therefore never come to appreciate.

Encourage yourself with this thought: the emotional battle is temporary, but *being an author is eternal*. Your words will eventually be immortalized in print, touching the lives of others through your written legacy long after your death. This great achievement won't be handed to you; you must first earn that right. The only thing that stands in your way is the blank page (or screen) in front of you.

From blank page to finished manuscript

In the previous chapter, I laid out the five specific ways I prepare for each writing project. In this chapter, I want to share with you how to write your manuscript from start to finish.

1. Create a writing schedule.

   As you can probably tell, I take writing books very seriously. This is because I genuinely care about the reader and the possible impact I can have on their lives. When I take on a new book project, I mentally enter what I call "book-writing mode." Essentially, I allow the project to consume my life until it is completed. My spare time becomes one of three activities: writing, researching, or thinking. This extreme level of focus for a short period of time allows me to harness the power of momentum to finish my books efficiently and quickly.

   I'm not suggesting that you should duplicate my over-the-top writing schedule. I am suggesting that you *create a writing schedule for yourself and stick to it*. No matter what time you decide to write or in what location, the key is to make it a daily habit. The practice of daily writing is the most important habit an author can develop. It is the mark of the serious writer and proof of your commitment to make a difference. Adopting this habit will take you further than anything else I could recommend.

   Some authors set out to write a specific number of pages every day and others strive for a predetermined word count. My goal is to simply *show up*. Every day, without fail, I show up. I choose to be present in the moment and write. Whatever progress this yields for the day, I'm fine with that. This means that some days I will be inspired to create some of the most beautiful writing I've ever produced. Other days, I will stare at my computer screen wondering why I ever attempted to write a book.

Whether you choose to dedicate your mornings to working on your book or your lunch breaks at work, show up every day and trust that the writing will take care of itself.

2. Create a tentative book title.

   The first sentence I write for each new book project is always a tentative book title. I say "tentative" because it usually grows and changes before I finish the book. Having a book title in place *before* I write helps me stay on topic and inspires me to write. I like to type it up in big letters and print it out to resemble a book cover that sits beside me on my desk as I write.

   The first piece of writing your readers absorb from you is your book title. It should be easy to read, easy to say, and easy to communicate to others. When you look at the cover of a nonfiction book, you'll notice that it usually has a title and a subtitle. The title acts as the attention grabber and the subtitle explains what the book is about. Here are a few examples from my previous books:

   - *Visionary: Making a difference in a world that needs YOU!*

- *Cultivate: 4 Principles to help your mate recognize and fulfill her potential*
- *Do These Five: 5 Simple tips for permanent, sustainable weight-loss*
- *BROKE: 4 Money mistakes holding you back from financial freedom and the life of your dreams!*

Here are a few examples from books in my personal library:

- *Speak to Win: How to Present with Power in Any Situation*
- *On Writing Well: The Classic Guide to Writing Nonfiction*
- *Winning with People: Discover the People Principles that Work for You Every Time*

There are also nonfiction books that don't use a subtitle because the title explains its contents.

- *How to Win Friends and Influence People*
- *The 7 Habits of Highly Effective People*

Some authors can't begin to write without first having a title for their project. Others choose to create a title when the project is finished. When you decide to create your title is a matter of personal preference. Do whatever allows you to create more effectively.

3. Create an outline.

Creating an outline is basically planning your book in advance. It is creating a roadmap for how your book will flow and take shape. An outline isn't meant to be a concrete template for your writing. You don't want it to act as a prison for your creativity. The purpose of an outline is to make your writing easier by serving as a loose guide for your content.

Once you have your outline in place, you have the foundational building blocks of your message. If you find yourself not able to construct an outline of your message, this may be a signal you are not ready to begin writing just yet. Spend more time assessing the needs of your ideal reader, reading books similar to your topic, and writing notes in your journal – as discussed in the chapter on pre-writing.

To create your outline, begin with a brain dump. A brain dump is the act of transferring the knowledge in your mind on a particular subject to another place of storage – which in this case will be a sheet of paper. Find a quiet environment where you can be alone to examine your thoughts. Bring a pen and your journal. Take out a clean sheet of paper and write the tentative title you created or the subject of your book on the top of the paper.

Now, write everything that comes to your mind about your topic on the page. Continue to write until you run out of ideas. The goal is to take everything from your brain and dump it on the page without placing any judgment on what you have written. Don't forget to read through your journal and transfer any important ideas from there to your brain dump.

Look over what you have written and organize them into main ideas or categories. Each main idea is a potential chapter in your book; what you have written under each main idea is potential content for that chapter. Once you have organized your chapters into a logical flow, you are ready to begin writing.

4. Write your first draft.

    Start with the first point on your outline and begin to write! Expand on each point in your outline by using facts, stories, quotes, and dialogue. Don't focus on editing your work or creating the perfect book in this draft. You will polish and fine tune your work in subsequent drafts. The purpose of your first draft is simple: TO GET YOUR THOUGHTS ON PAPER.

    Keep in mind that the easiest way to write your book is to approach it as a conversation with the ideal reader. Training myself to approach writing in this way has been the most helpful tool for increasing my productivity.

5. Write your second draft.

    Set your first draft aside for a day or so and then begin to re-read your work. The second draft can be very discouraging if you allow it to be. Don't beat yourself up over all the obvious mistakes in your writing. Understand that this is a part of the creation process. Here are some things to look for as you go through your writing:

    - Words or sentences that are out of sequence or redundant.
    - Basic punctuation, spelling, and grammar mistakes.

- The flow or rhythm of your writing.
- The overuse of words you use to express yourself. Economize your writing. Ask yourself if you can say the same thing with fewer words.

6. Write your third draft.

    Before you write your third draft, you want to let your manuscript sit for a week or so. This is because you want fresh eyes for your final revision. As you engage in the repetitious cycle of writing, reading, and rewriting your manuscript, you'll notice that you begin to memorize it. Your mind will insert words into sentences that are not actually on the page or insert meaning into paragraphs that were not properly communicated to the reader. This is why you should step away from your work for one week before you begin writing your final draft. This is also why you should have a professional editor review your work before it goes to the printer.

    When I read through my final draft, I am primarily looking for the clarity of my message. I ask myself these questions: "Did I say what I set out to say? Is my message clear? Do my readers need to know anything else?" Once I verify that I have communicated my message to the best of my ability, I send it to a professional editor for review.

7. Hire a professional editor.

    The last step in the writing process is to have your manuscript professionally edited. A poorly edited book communicates unprofessionalism and decreases the credibility of the author along with the message as a whole. Editors perform an invaluable service to writers; they are the unsung heroes of the publishing world. No matter how much I self-edit my writing and believe I have polished it beyond correction, I am always humbled when I receive my manuscript from the editor with a considerable number of errors.

Thankfully, professional editors are easy to come by because the internet has given us access to a global market of freelancers. There are many companies that allow freelancers to offer their services online. One of the most popular, and the company I personally use, is UpWork.com. Their website is fairly simple to navigate and each freelancer I have worked with completed quality work at a fair price.

To begin on Upwork, you'll need to create a free account. Once you do that you can use the search bar to find professional editing services. You'll be able to browse profiles of freelancers at different price points and levels of skill. Once you find an editor at the skill level and price point you desire, you'll send them your manuscript for the first round of edits. From my experience, it usually takes three rounds of edits to get the job done. It could take more depending on how large your book is and how much work your editor needs to do. Look over each revision the editor makes carefully. You are hiring them to make editorial suggestions about your work, but you still have the final say in the end.

Once your editing process is finalized and complete, congratulations, you are an author!

Chapter 4
HOW TO PUBLISH YOUR BOOK

The world of publishing has changed drastically. The cost of entry is no longer writing proposals, tracking down literary agents, or forking over thousands of dollars to printing companies. The ease of modern publishing has leveled the playing field, empowering anyone with an internet connection and a desire to see their words in print the ability to be published.

I can assure you that publishing your book is quite easy compared to actually writing your book. You will recognize the truth in that statement when your book is completed. If you've read this far, you know how to write a nonfiction book. In this final chapter, I want to give you an overview of the do-it-yourself publishing process.

1. Commit to quality.

    Thousands of books are self-published each year and many of them are of sub-par quality. Each time this second-rate material is released into the marketplace, it reinforces a popular stigma that self-published books are inferior to books that have been published traditionally.

    When you decide to self-publish your book, you are taking complete ownership of the finished product. Take pride in what you put out to the world. Make a commitment to producing quality.

2. Choose your publishing platform.

    There are many well-known self-publishing platforms such as Lulu, Lighting Source, and Smashwords. My personal preference has always been Amazon's publishing platform, Kindle Direct Publishing or KDP.com. Their service is free, requires no prior experience, and they provide written and video instructions that walk you through the requirements to publish with them.

    As a self-publisher, you are in the driver's seat of your book production process. You decide the size of your book, the price of your book, and even the marketing information for your book. These publishing platforms don't make decisions for you; they only provide the infrastructure for you to execute your own.

3. Make your manuscript look like a book.

    The next step in the publishing process is to have your manuscript properly formatted for publishing.

Formatting refers to the layout and interior design of your manuscript's pages. This process is what makes the words you've written look professional and attractive to the reader.

Unless you have experience in this area, I suggest that you hire someone to format your book professionally. A good formatter will take your boring Microsoft Word document and make it look like a bestseller worthy of its place in a major bookstore. Having your book professionally formatted is just as important as having it professionally edited; use caution when you decide who will perform this task for you. Your goal is to self-publish your book without it being obvious that it has been self-published. One of the signs of an inferior book is improper formatting of interior pages.

There are many blogs and YouTube videos that will show you how to format your book for free. There is even a formatting template with instructions on my publishing platform of choice, kdp.com. I know many authors who have formatted their own books and they have turned out great, but this is not something I have had the patience to learn. Each time I need formatting work done I turn to the freelancers at Upwork.com. The process I outlined to find and collaborate with an editor in the previous chapter is also the process I use to work with a professional formatter.

4. Decide on your cover design.

 Your cover is literally the face of your book. It visually communicates the tone, feel, and quality of your manuscript. Everything – from the colors, the font size, and the images you use – says something about what may be inside your book. Your book cover always sends a message to the marketplace. Smart authors are intentional about the message their book cover communicates.

Ask yourself these questions:

- What message do you want your book to send?
- Should it have a clean, bare look with minimal writing?
- Should it have bright, vibrant, inviting colors with lots of writing?
- Should it communicate humor in some way?
- Should it have images? And if so, what will those images communicate?

Do some research on book covers in your genre. How do they look? Are any of them similar to how you envision your cover to be? Before I have my book cover designed, I like to find four or five covers I really like and present them to my designer as a catalyst to build on. I found that supplying a physical representation of something I like makes it easier for my designer to create something unique but in line with my specific desires.

5. Upload your files.

    Upload the finalized digital files of your book cover and manuscript to your publishing platform. Once your files are uploaded they will go through a preliminary check to make sure they meet specific guidelines. When this phase is complete it will enter the proofing process. Proofing your book means that you are reviewing the final copy of your work before it is sent to your readers.

There are two proofing options to choose from: digital and physical. Digital proofing is when you review and approve the finished book file online. Physical proofing is when you have a physical copy mailed to your home for an in-person approval. I recommend using both options for your first book to do a thorough check and get familiar with what to look for during the proofing process. After that, you will probably only need the digital proofing option.

6. Publish in multiple formats.

   One of the worst publishing decisions you can make is to only publish your book in one format. When you only have your book available in one format, you do yourself, your readers, and your bank account a great disservice. Everyone has their preferred way of consuming books. Some readers like digital books, others like physical books, and many will only listen to audio books. You want to be equipped to supply the most popular preferences of the marketplace.

   One of the surprising things about having your book available in multiple formats is that some readers will connect with your message so much that they will purchase it in all available formats. This means that one customer could potentially give you three book sales instead of only one, just because they had the opportunity to do so.

Your e-book and paperback versions can be produced at kdp.com but your audio book has slightly different steps. ACX.COM is my website of choice when it comes to audio book production. Just like kdp.com, they are owned by Amazon and are essentially a company built to help people self-publish and distribute their audio books. They make the process pretty seamless for authors and narrators to team up and produce a great audio book. They also teach you best practices for narrating your own audio book if you choose to do so. After your audio book is finished it will be distributed through iTunes, Audible, and Amazon.com.

7. Learn how to successfully launch and market your book.

   The success of your book will be directly correlated to your marketing and promotion skills. People will not find and purchase your book simply because it is well written and has a great message. Most authors spend hours of time and effort on their book only for it to fall into obscurity soon after it is released.

   There are only two reasons why this would happen.

   1. There is something wrong with the message.
   2. There is something wrong with the marketing of the message.

   You must consistently and actively participate in the marketing of your book for it to have the impact you desire. It will be uncomfortable, and it is hard work, but it is necessary.

I don't write these words as an expert on marketing and promotion. This is an area of business I am still in the process of mastering. There are many excellent marketing and book promotion experts in the world of publishing. Here are a few I recommend.

- Tim Grahl

    Tim has two books every author should read. One is called *Your First 1000 Copies*; the other is called *Book Launch Blueprint.*

- Brendon Burchard

    Brendon has a world-renowned business focused on helping people make a living from becoming a subject matter expert. You can find him at ExpertsAcademy.com

- Tom Corson Knowles

    Tom is the bestselling author of more than 20 self-published books. He is also an expert at marketing and promoting self-published books. You can find him at TKCPublishing.com

CONCLUSION

I am grateful you have invested your valuable time into reading this book. My hope is that you understand how valuable your message is to the world and feel confident that you can move forward with writing your book. I know with absolute certainty that you have what it takes to give the world the gift of your book. Your potential readers are waiting on you!

**If this book has helped you in any way, please head over to <u>amazon.com</u> and leave a review.
I would love to hear your thoughts.**

ABOUT THE AUTHOR

Tony Rogers Jr. is an entrepreneur, teacher and founder of The Visionary Society - a global training company dedicated to equipping visionaries with the tools and strategies they need to make a difference in the world. He is a proud native of Dayton, Ohio the birthplace of aviation.

OTHER BOOKS FROM THE AUTHOR

The Visionary Library is an ongoing series of books dedicated to helping visionary thinkers create positive change the world. You have just finished the second book in this series. The first book in this series is titled: *Visionary: Making a difference in a world that needs YOU!* Look for this book on amazon.com.

I also write about finances, relationships, weight loss, and other topics under the pen name, Maurice Rogers Jr.

Printed in Great Britain
by Amazon